INTENTIONAL LIVING

INTENTIONAL LIVING

VALARI KNIGHT BOSTON

Published by Spines
ISBN 979-8-89569-903-4

CONTENTS

ACKNOWLEDGMENTS

In response to the profound urgency I feel bestowed upon me by God, coupled with the multitude of voices that have prophetically urged me forward —"there's a treasure of wisdom locked within you, now is the time to unlock it and share it with the world"—I have finally set pen to paper. My life's mission unfurls before me, a sacred calling to prayerfully reach out and ignite inspiration in the hearts of those who desire guidance, for the wisdom I've held within me for far too long now begs to be released.

As I embark on this transformative journey, I am steadily letting go of the fears and doubts that have tethered me, making space for clarity and purpose. To my cherished family and my covenant friends, know that your love and support are the pillars upon which I stand.

To my daughter Jaime, my Sage Warrior — you are an unparalleled source of motivation, a shining beacon whose light illuminates my path with your unwavering belief in my potential.

To God, I am eternally grateful for the vision and inspiration you have endowed upon me, for the trials and tribulations that have forged my spirit and prepared me to stride boldly down the path toward becoming the woman you designed me to be. Thank you for the sacred opportunity to listen closely to your whispers and for the chance to touch lives—may my words resonate with all who seek
solace and enlightenment.

INTRODUCTION

I'm not sure how it's been for you, but life has this knack for slinging curveballs our way, forcing us to stop and reflect. I've experienced this more times than I care to admit, stepping back from the passions and purposes that I believe I was truly meant to embrace. There have been challenges that struck me with unexpected force, leaving me breathless and disoriented. Such trials have often led me off course, allowing the noise of external distractions and deceitful ambitions to overshadow my true purpose, steering me far from the divine path I was destined to walk. In the end, I come to understand that trials impose challenges, and these challenges cultivate testing; it's through testing that we uncover perseverance, and from this perseverance, we ultimately forge a deeper maturity.

This book aims to forge that deeper maturity and reposition you with God's intentions for your life. It is designed to guide you back to the track that God laid out for you from the moment you entered this world, encouraging you to live with intention and clarity. Understanding that intentional living means existing with purpose—actively, deliberately, and for a reason—is crucial. That purpose is fundamentally about answering the call God has placed on your life. The purpose speaks to the movement not just the moment. While you might not fully grasp what that demand necessitates at this moment, I urge you to engage with God today, to explore your identity and the unique purpose you were born to achieve.

Just think for a moment: consider how utterly unique you truly are. Of all the individuals you could have been, God chose for you to be— you! You are extraordinary, exceptional, and singular. There resides within you a magnificent purpose just waiting to be unveiled. Let's embark on this quest together!

As you embark on the journey through this book, I invite you to carry these crucial words—intent, intention, and intentionality—into your exploration. Each term holds profound weight, and understanding their application is essential. When we delve into the word intention, I urge you to expand your perception beyond the surface.

The definition of *intent* encompasses not just what one desires to accomplish but also embodies a sense of purpose, a conscious formulation of thought that drives action. It speaks to a level of thoughtfulness and deliberateness that can shape our paths. Now, let's consider the concept of intent; it is more than mere thought. It is the result of focused attention directed towards a particular object of knowledge or understanding. Can your mind embrace the exciting potential of embarking on a novel endeavor? The word intention provides a mere glimpse into that world, suggesting the expansive horizon of what you aim to manifest. What aspirations flicker in the corners of your mind?

Moving to the word objective, we touch on the tangible—what is concrete and within reach. Within these pages, you will unearth keys designed to guide us in leading lives filled with purpose and concrete goals.

The ultimate objective? To chart a course that brings us ever closer to those aspirations. Meanwhile, the term design adds another layer, indicating that intention is not happenstance but a calculated and orchestrated plan of action. It delineates the 'how' of our journeys, setting a framework through which we can attain our ambitions.

Finally, consider the word goal, which evokes something that requires sustained effort and resolute determination to achieve. Achieving your dreams is seldom easy; it often demands relentless perseverance through trials and tribulations. Yet, it is precisely through this struggle—through grit and tenacity—that we not only address our obstacles but ultimately claim our rewards.

As you engage with this material, let these concepts resonate within you, as they hold the keys to unlocking your potential and realizing your deepest desires.

To further understand intent read the following.

Are not two sparrows sold for a penny? Yet not one of them will fall to the ground outside your Father's care. Matthew 10:29 (NIV)

Jesus' intent in this verse is not to say that God watches over parrows but rather to affirm that God watches over his children.

So don't be afraid; you are worth more than many sparrows. (v.31)

God's intention is the Word of God, the Bible. Reading the Bible daily helps you to understand God's intention for your life.

Learning God's intention reveals your purpose. God values your life and wants you to enjoy your life with purpose and intent.

God wants you to have the full understanding of his love and his purpose for your life.

How do you want to live?

1

WHAT IS INTENTIONAL LIVING?

Intentional Living embodies a profound commitment to embracing your life with a resolute PURPOSE.

Have you taken the time to discover your true purpose?

Today, let us boldly declare and decree that:

It is a conscious choice to lead a life filled with intention and meaning.

It's about navigating your days with deliberate action.

Let us strategize together to live for God with a heartfelt intention.

What aspects of your life ignite that fire of intentionality within you?

MY NOTES

MY NOTES

2

I WANT TO BE INTENTIONAL ABOUT

…witnessing the light of Jesus reflected in my daily actions, leading others to glimpse His grace through my life.

…embracing the call to treat each soul I encounter with the compassion and love that Christ so deeply desires for all His children.

…journeying ever deeper into the richness of the gospel of Jesus Christ, allowing its truths to transform my heart and shape my path.

…committing to live a life anchored in the eternal WORD of God, letting its teachings guide my thoughts and decisions.

…directing my FOCUS toward the incredible future that God has lovingly designed for me, a future brimming with hope and purpose!

Now, that's what I call INTENTIONAL LIVING, a deliberate dance with destiny!

INTENTIONAL LIVING...

This is the reason why we were created, to serve a purpose far greater than ourselves.

After all this, there is only one thing to say: have reverence for God, and obey his commands, because this is all that human beings were created for.
Ecclesiastes 12:13 Good News.

After you awaken each day, what visions stir within you? What dreams call to you from the depths of your consciousness? Today presents a canvas of limitless possibilities, and the brush is in your hands. What path will you choose to explore, and what intentions will you set forth to guide you on this journey?

Embrace the day, for it is a new chapter waiting to be created.
What is your intent today?

MY NOTES

Have you ever awakened with the first light of dawn spilling golden hues across your room, feeling a restless urge clawing at your heart, compelling you to seize the day in an entirely new way?

What swirling thoughts danced through your mind at that very moment—how fervently did you yearn to reinvent yourself, to take a turn down uncharted paths?
Did you wake up and declare, with steadfast conviction, that today marks the onset of an exciting new chapter in your life?

With each heartbeat, did you feel the promise of transformation whispering sweetly in your ear, urging you to embrace the possibilities that lay just beyond the horizon?

Put those declarations down on the following page.
What is it that's gnawing at your heart?
Capture what you truly feel.
Let's continue writing.
How do you begin your morning routine?
Are you driven by purpose?
Do you manage your hours with intention?
Is your focus sharply set on achieving results?
Do you practice mindfulness throughout your day?
How do you close out your evening?
Reflect on these inquiries and jot down your reflections.

BE INTENTIONAL!

PRAY

MY NOTES

3

____

EMBRACING THE DAWN

Here I am, fully awake! What a miraculous gift this moment is! The very first step I should
take is to express my heartfelt gratitude to God for allowing me the blessing of another day.
I ought to navigate my thoughts towards his endless goodness, grace, and mercy, right? Yet,
somehow, my mind drifts impulsively to a myriad of distractions... the unsettling nuances of
the news that played before bed, the bustling activities of my children, and the ever-growing
concern about whether my grandchildren have been flourishing in their studies. It's as if
I've unwittingly opened a floodgate of thoughts, and now my mind is racing off
in every conceivable direction.
Upon awakening, my contemplation may lazily shift from the pressing tasks on my agenda
to an overwhelming analysis of how on earth I will tackle any of it effectively. My calendar,
usually a kaleidoscope of responsibilities demanding my unwavering attention, seems
daunting as an avalanche of obligations.
Recently, however, I've made a conscious choice to set those burdens aside, to let them rest
on a metaphorical shelf.

It is all too effortless to find oneself mentally frayed, racing between a multitude of thoughts
moment by moment. Thus, we must be delightfully deliberate and intentional with each
passing hour, crafting our day with purpose and clarity amidst the clutter of our busy lives.

Getting started

Pray About Where You Want to Begin

TALK TO THE FATHER AND BE INTENTIONAL ABOUT YOUR DAY

MY NOTES

4

FOCUSED

Beginning your day with discernment can illuminate the path ahead, casting a gentle light that guides your thoughts and intentions. It serves as an anchor, allowing you to navigate the complexities of life with clarity and purpose. As you rise, remember the importance of reaching out to God, seeking guidance on the when, where, and how of each step you take. This sacred dialogue invites understanding and prepares you to embrace the unfolding journey
with an open heart.

Whether you turn to the right or to the left, your ears will hear a voice behind you, saying, "This is the way; walk in it." Isaiah 30:21

Seeking guidance from God is not just important; it is fundamentally crucial for leading a purposeful and intentional life. In the grand tapestry of existence, where each thread represents a choice, the act of asking for divine direction offers clarity amidst the chaos. It transforms our wandering thoughts into focused intentions, anchoring us through the stormy seas of uncertainty. By calling upon the divine wisdom, we align ourselves with a greater plan, allowing our lives to unfold in ways that resonate with deep meaning and significance.

In this dialogue with the Almighty, we find not only direction but also the courage to embark on the paths laid out before us, illuminating our journeys with discernment and grace.

The name of the LORD is a fortified tower; the righteous run to it and are safe. Proverbs 18:10

In all your ways acknowledge Him, and He will make your paths straight.
Proverbs 3:6

He guides the humble in what is right and teaches them His way.
Psalm 25:9

He is my steadfast love and my fortress, my stronghold and my deliverer. He is my shield, in whom I take refuge, who subdues peoples under me.
Psalm 144:2

5

MOTIVATION

YOUR REWARD COMES NOT FROM MEN, BUT FROM GOD.

Slaves, obey your earthly masters in everything; and do it, not only when their eye is on you and to win their favor, but with sincerity of heart and reverence for the Lord. Whatever you do, work it all with your heart, as working for the Lord, not for men. Colossians 3:22-23

What truly compels me to see through a task until its end is the tantalizing reward that waits on the other side of completion. Much like how we drag ourselves to the gym day after day, grimacing at the rigorous exercises that are before is, we find ourselves secretly resenting them. Yet, as the weeks pass and our bodies begin to transform, we start to embrace the inevitable outcome—the strength, stamina, and sculpted form that emerge as a testament to our perseverance. We learn to love the results, and the journey turns from a burden into a badge of honor. Spiritual maturity mirrors this process remarkably well. It's far more than a mere checkpoint; it's an evolving journey, an ongoing conditioning of the soul, rather than a final destination awaiting our arrival.
There are moments along this path when we resist the mandate to learn something new or embrace the intricate lessons life throws our way.

Still, as we inhale each moment and absorb the wisdom found in sacred texts as well as our daily experiences, we ignite gleams of hope. This hope leads us closer to a profound connection with Christ. In this unfolding journey, we truly become better versions of ourselves. The transformation that occurs within begins to reflect outwardly, and suddenly we find ourselves inspired! We start to envision a life that is richer and deeper through knowing Him more intimately. The best way to grasp this is to remind ourselves of the glorious day that awaits us—a day when we will know Him fully, when our spiritual walk (or, perhaps, our grand race) will find its fulfilling conclusion. So, let this thought fuel your spirit: strive to know Christ more deeply and embrace the journey with open hearts and eager minds.I must be intentional about my practices.

My heart finds its deepest motivation in the sacred pages of the Word of God. Each verse resonates within me like a divine echo, urging me onwards in my journey of faith. The teachings and promises contained within guide my actions and illuminate my path, reminding me of a greater purpose that transcends my earthly existence. In moments of doubt or hardship, it is this holy scripture that reignites my spirit, instilling hope and inspiring me to live according to His will. Embracing His words fuels my passion and shapes my character, leading me to strive for goodness and grace in all that I do.

WHAT MOTIVATES ME?

What truly motivates you, deep down in the recesses of your mind? Is it the unwavering pursuit of success that pushes you to rise with the dawn, fueled by dreams and ambitions larger than life itself? Or perhaps it's the whisper of curiosity, the longing to explore the uncharted territories of knowledge and creativity, propelling you into realms untouched by the average soul. The heart beats to the rhythm of desire and necessity, where each pulse resonates with the ideals we hold dear. Consider for a moment the tapestry of experiences that layer our lives like a fine quilt—each stitch represents a moment of inspiration, a spark igniting our passions. Maybe it's the yearning for connection and understanding that draws you toward meaningful relationships, or the relentless chase after answers to profound questions that gnaw at your spirit. Everyone has their own compass, guiding them through the vast sea of choices and chances that life presents. And in this journey, the true essence of what drives you emerges like a morning sun breaking through the clouds, illuminating your path with purpose. Whether it's ambition, curiosity, connection, or a quest for knowledge, recognize that these motivations intertwine, creating a unique narrative that is solely yours. Cherish it, for within lies the heartbeat of your existence, the fuel that can launch you into extraordinary adventures yet to come.

6

RELEASING THE PAST

Reflecting on the past can often serve to pull us backward, diverting our focus away from the opportunities that lie ahead! It's time to cease this backward glance! Be purposeful in shedding the weight of past negativity
that clings to you like a shadow!

Have you truly released the lingering chains of the past,
or do you still find yourself ensnared?
Are you held captive by past wounds, still feeling the sting from those long-gone moments or toxic relationships?

Are you confined by the limitations that once defined you, shackled to former beliefs that no longer serve your journey?

Do you bear the heavy burden of past mistakes, allowing guilt
and regret to stifle your growth?

Now is the moment to seek liberation through prayer; reach out for the strength to break free and embrace the vibrant future that eagerly awaits!

Let's reflect on the story of Lot's wife found in Genesis 19.

Angels came to visit the cities of Sodom and Gomorrah and carried a serious warning from the Lord preparing to destroy the cities. These angels urged Lot and his family to leave immediately and in doing so told them to "flee for their lives and not to look back or to stop anywhere in the plain or you will be swept away."(v.17)

Lot's wife and daughters heeded the urgent command of the angels, their hearts pounding as they fled the harrowing embrace of the burning rain of sulphur that consumed the sin-filled cities behind them. With each frantic step, freedom beckoned, yet Lot's wife found herself mired in a swirl of memories—a kaleidoscope of her past life filled with glimmers of joy, sorrow, and the all-too-enticing familiarity of what she was leaving behind.

Torn between the promise of salvation and the haunting pull of nostalgia, she turned her gaze back, unable to sever the chains of her former existence. In that fateful moment of hesitation, she transformed into a pillar of salt, a haunting testament to the cost of her disobedience.

Sin binds you with invisible shackles, anchoring your spirit to fleeting pleasures that once felt so vibrant and enticing. It whispers sweet lies, convincing you that clinging to the past is safer than embracing the unknown future. This insidious force stunts your growth, halting your evolution as a person—a betrayal of your true potential.

The tragic fate of Lot's wife serves as a stark reminder; in Genesis 19, her lingering glance sealed her fate, leaving her forever estranged from the possibility of becoming who God meant for her to be. In her moment of temptation, despite the angels' desperate warnings, she couldn't shake free from the siren song of her sins.
The path to liberation lay before her, offered by divine mercy in the form of destruction—a mercy meant to usher her into a new beginning. But still, she looked back, caught in a web of regret, unable to release the burdens of her past as the flames of judgment flared brightly behind her.

I recall a profound message that Bishop T.D. Jakes preached that resonated with me a few years back, one that delved deeply into the notion of carrying the past as if it were an ever-present burden. The message revolved around a person, burdened by their sins, whose struggles were artfully compared to the weight of a lifeless carcass that clung to their very being. This carcass, grotesque and decaying, trailed behind them like an unshakeable shadow, a grim reminder of the mistakes that haunted their every step. Over time, as the carcass rotted away, it became not just a weight to bear but a source of foulness, permeating the air and adhering to the person, intertwining their essence with its death.

Who, in their right mind, would willingly carry the foul stench of decay? Yet, there are those among us who seem to do just that, unknowingly festooned with the remnants of past transgressions, oblivious to the odor that signals their burden. It's a cautionary tale—a vivid metaphor urging us to shed our burdens before they anchor us to the past in a most unpleasant way.

Release that thing and LET IT GO!

Dead things are meant to be buried, yet even the most dedicated gardener understands that within the decay of some lifeless remains lies the potential for new growth. As you carefully sift through the remnants of what no longer serves you, take a moment to acknowledge the lessons encased within
these carcasses of your past.

Bury them deep in the fertile soil of your memory, where their essence can mingle with the earth, enriching it, transforming decay into nourishment. Let them cultivate resilience and purpose, nurturing the blossoms of success that await in your future. Only through this cycle of death and rebirth can you truly flourish, as the promise of new beginnings takes root, drawing energy from the very things you've let go.

Pray

MY NOTES

Do we allow the past to fade into obscurity, shrouded in shadows, or do we confront it head-on, examining every nuance, every misstep, knowing that it molds our present? Throughout our journey, we often discover that some of the most profound lessons are etched in the annals of our past, particularly those arising from our failures. These lessons are inescapable. Every misstep offers a treasure trove of wisdom. Yet, have you considered that our ability to reflect on our history not only shapes who we are but also steers our course as we venture into the uncertain terrain of the future? Indeed, our triumphs illuminate our path just as brightly. What could be more fulfilling than basking in the glow of an accomplishment born of hard work and perseverance?

As we sift through memories, I pray that these reflections serve as signposts, guiding us in our relationship with others. Accessing the archives of our past is a healthy exercise, one that should empower us, rather than allowing it to dictate the blueprint of our destiny. In essence, the failures we cling to do not have to haunt us relentlessly, reminding us of what went wrong.

As a Christian, you are gifted with the grace of renewal through Christ Jesus, a continual source of hope.

Your existence embodies the promise that he sacrificed everything so that you might embrace life in its fullest form. When I take a moment to survey my own life, I am struck by the numerous second chances bestowed upon me by Jesus' enduring love. He gently nudges me to remember that while my list of mistakes may be daunting, there is renewal in acknowledging the critical essence of having Him as an anchor in my life. Each blunder paves the way for understanding, revealing the beauty of grace that redefines who I am.

As I reflect on my life, I cannot overlook the series of decisions I've made that teetered on the brink of calamity. Yet, through each misstep, I have witnessed God's unwavering hand guiding me through turbulent waters to land me safely in the present day. It's precisely this divine navigation that has instilled in me the crucial understanding of why placing my faith in Him as my central FOCUS is not just important but essential to my existence today.

Looking back at those years that seemed squandered, I could easily succumb to despair, branding myself a failure. However, I choose a different path—one that moves me towards the divine calling that God has set before me. It's on this vibrant journey, laden with lessons and growth, that I find myself thanking
Him daily for His grace and wisdom.

Each lesson learned and every trial faced has carved out a stronger version of myself, one that thrives on the resilience born from past struggles.

I consciously opt not to linger in the shadows of regret; those memories serve more as stepping stones rather than chains binding me to the past. Yes, I remember those moments; they are stitched into the fabric of who I am, but I choose not to dwell there. Instead, my heart soars with excitement for what lies ahead.

With unwavering determination, I INTENTIONALLY FOCUS FORWARD, with the fervent belief that brighter days and new beginnings await, as long as I keep my gaze set on Him.

MY NOTES

7

HE IS MY COVERING

Throughout my formative years in elementary school, art classes became a sanctuary for my budding creativity. We immersed ourselves in a world where we could paint, draw, and create using every medium imaginable—crayons, acrylics, watercolor, and even the messy pastels that left smudges on our fingers and clothes.

From the innocent days of kindergarten through to the slightly more sophisticated fifth grade, we were required to don cover-ups. These makeshift aprons, typically our fathers' well-worn shirts, enveloped us in a comforting embrace, protecting our young bodies from neck to knees against the chaos that art could bring.

I vividly remember the feel of one of my dad's old shirts draping over me in art class; it was not just a garment but an experience. As I stood at the easel, the fabric alive with memories of his scent—sharp notes of English Leather or Old Spice mixed with the faint aroma of paint—I felt a profound sense of safety. In that shirt, I could freely smear paint, glue, or even sprinkle glitter without the worry of soiling my school clothes. It was liberating; I was truly protected! Today, my affinity for creativity continues, and I often find myself wearing various aprons in the kitchen and studio to keep my clothes safe from unintended artistic adventure.

In a delightful way, this simple childhood memory speaks volumes about the intentional protection offered by God. Just as that old, oversized shirt shielded me from the mess of my creative pursuits, God's care envelops us, offering protection against life's trials and tribulations. Even while wearing my dad's shirt, I discovered that I could dive into creative chaos, emerging unscathed and unharmed. God operates in a similar fashion; He enables us to navigate through challenges and difficult circumstances without letting them tarnish our lives. Through our struggles, He stands like that old shirt, ensuring we are shielded from the damaging effects of the world, allowing us to emerge stronger and more resilient.

HE IS OUR COVERING

Have confidence in your leaders and submit to their authority, because they keep watch over you as those who must give an account. Do this so that their work will be a joy, not a burden, for that would be of no benefit to you. Hebrews 13:17 NIV

"You are a hiding place for me; you preserve me from trouble; you surround me with shouts of deliverance. Selah Psalm 32:7 ESV

"He will cover you with his feathers, and under his wings you will find refuge; his faithfulness will be your shield and rampart. Psalm 91:4 NIV

"Because he holds fast to me in love, I will deliver him; I will protect him, because he knows my name." Psalm 91:14 ESV

"But the Lord is faithful. He will establish you and guard you against the evil one."
2 Thessalonians 3:3 NIV

For I know the plans I have for you," declares the Lord, "plans to prosper you and not to harm you, plans to give you hope and a future.
Jeremiah 29:11

MY NOTES

8

INTENTIONALLY FOCUSED FORWARD!

Looking Back Stunts. Our Spiritual Growth

We have much to say about this, but it is hard to make it clear to you because you no longer try to understand. In fact, though by this time you ought to be teachers, you need someone to teach you the elementary truths of God's word all over again. You need milk, not solid food! Anyone who lives on milk, being still an infant, is not acquainted with the teaching about righteousness. But solid food is for the mature, who by constant use have trained themselves to distinguish good from evil. Hebrews 5:11-14

In the early days of our existence, when we were but infants, we drift through each day unburdened, wrapped in a cocoon of innocence, blissfully unaware of the complexities that lie ahead. Yet as the years accumulate, our perspective shifts dramatically; we begin to glimpse the intricate tapestry of life that unfolds before us. Each moment transforms from a fleeting experience into a vessel of expectation, laden with the weight of understanding and anticipation. We find ourselves gazing toward the horizon, where dreams and possibilities intertwine, ushering in a profound sense of hope.

Our journey becomes one of conscious discovery as we navigate the vast expanse of our aspirations, firmly focusing forward, eager to embrace the unfolding chapters of our lives, each filled with the promise of what lies ahead.

Leaving the weight of our past behind us opens the door to a realm of self-awareness—an illuminating journey that propels us toward a brighter future. Embracing the knowledge of our intrinsic value and self-worth empowers us to stand resilient and confident, ready to claim the abundant promises that were laid before us by the hand of God. With each step, we cultivate a deeper understanding of who we are, not as the sum of our experiences, but as unique individuals crafted with purpose. This awareness casts away doubts and fears, allowing us to march forward with faith, anchored in the belief that our destiny is intertwined with divine plans that flourish with hope and possibility.

"Since we've compiled this long and sorry record as sinners (both us and them) and proved that we are utterly incapable of living the glorious lives God wills for us, God did it for us. Out of sheer generosity he put us in right standing with himself. A pure gift. He got us out of the mess we're in and restored us to where he always wanted us to be. And he did it by means of Jesus Christ. God sacrificed Jesus on the altar of the world to clear that world of sin. Having faith in him sets us in the clear. God decided on this course of action in full view of the public - to set the world in the clear with himself through the sacrifice of Jesus, finally taking care of the sins, he had so patiently endured. This is not only clear, but it's now - this is current history! God sets things right. He also makes it possible for us to live in his rightness"
Romans 3:23-26 The Message

The Lord is my light and my salvation- whom shall, I fear? The Lord is the stronghold of my life- of whom shall I be afraid? When the wicked advance against me to devour me, it is my enemies and my foes who will stumble and fall. Though an army besiege me, my heart will not fear; though war break out against me, even then I will be confident. Psalm 18:2 NIV

Light, space, zest - that's God! So, with him on my side I'm fearless, afraid of no one and nothing. Psalm 27:1,3 The Message

For the Lord is your security. He will keep your foot from being caught in a trap. Proverbs 3:26 NLT

The name of the Lord is a strong fortress; the godly run to him and are safe. Proverbs 18:10

Address the lingering issues that have been a source of frustration and distraction in your life. By taking the time and effort to resolve these matters, you will find not only a newfound clarity of purpose but also a deeper sense of personal growth. The act of closing these chapters will not only sharpen your focus but also cultivate the qualities that make you a more compassionate and resilient individual. In this journey toward resolution, you will discover that each resolved conflict refines your character, leading you to a more enlightened and fulfilling existence.

We find ourselves in an extraordinary era, a time of unparalleled spiritual evolution, where the vibrations of the universe resonate with a call for deeper introspection and growth. This moment in history beckons each of us to rise to our higher selves and embrace our inner journeys, demanding your immediate and unwavering attention. The pathways to enlightenment are opening wider, inviting us to explore the boundless depths of our consciousness and the collective spirit that binds us all.

Pray About Those Issues

But now, O Lord, you are our Father; we are the clay, and you are our potter; we are all the work of your hand. Isaiah 64:8

MY NOTES

9

INTENTIONAL PURPOSE

Have you ever stopped for a moment to ponder the profound truth that you were intricately created for a specific purpose in this vast universe?

As I journeyed through the landscapes of my life, I began to uncover the beautiful tapestry of my purpose, woven together through prayer and steadfast faith. It became clear to me that my purpose is not just a personal endeavor; it is to worship and serve God wholeheartedly, aligning my heart's desires with His divine will.

In His infinite wisdom, He bestowed upon me the gifts and talents necessary to fulfill this sacred calling, guiding me gently along the path He designed for me.

So if you faithfully obey the commands I am giving you today—to love the Lord your God and to serve him with all your heart and with all your soul— then I will send rain on your land in its season, both autumn and spring rains, so that you may gather in your grain, new wine and olive oil. I will provide grass in the fields for your cattle, and you will eat and be satisfied. Deuteronomy 11:13-15

Do not work for food that perishes, but for food that endures to eternal life, which the Son of Man will give you. For on Him God the Father has placed His seal of approval. John 6:7

For my Father's will is that everyone who looks to the Son and believes in him shall have eternal life, and I will raise them up at the last day." John 6:40

For we are God's masterpiece. He has created us anew in Christ Jesus, so we can do the good things he planned for us long ago. Ephesians 2:10

So here's what I want you to do, God helping you: Take your everyday, ordinary life—your sleeping, eating, going-to-work, and walking-around life—and place it before God as an offering. Embracing what God does for you is the best thing you can do for him. Don't become so well-adjusted to your culture that you fit into it without even thinking. Instead, fix your attention on God. You'll be changed from the inside out. Readily recognize what he wants from you, and quickly respond to it. Unlike the culture around you, always dragging you down to its level of immaturity, God brings the best out of you, develops well-formed maturity in you.
Romans 12:1-2 The Message

The most extraordinary journey one can embark upon in the service of God is the profound realization that our very existence is intricately woven into the tapestry of His divine intentions. As beings fashioned in the very likeness of the Creator, we are endowed with the sacred mission to offer Him our heartfelt praise. In this beautiful act of worship, we discover that it is not merely an obligation but a source of unparalleled joy, fulfillment, and connection. For in our devotion, we find that He reciprocates with a grace that nourishes our spirits, tending to our every need and filling our lives with purpose and abundance. Through this divine exchange, we come to understand that in celebrating His glory, we simultaneously embrace our own unique purpose on this earthly journey.

Shout joyfully to the LORD, all the earth.

Serve the LORD with gladness;
Come before Him with joyful singing.

Know that the LORD Himself is God.

It is He who has made us, and not we ourselves.

We are His people and the sheep of His pasture.

Enter His gates with thanksgiving
And His courts with praise.

Give thanks to Him, bless His name.

Psalm 100:1-4

Lord, Show me My Purpose

10

PERSEVERE

A CALL TO PERSEVERE IN FAITH

Therefore, brothers and sisters, since we have confidence to enter the Most Holy Place by the blood of Jesus, by a new and living way opened for us through the curtain, that is, his body, and since we have a great priest over the house of God, let us draw near to God with a sincere heart and with the full assurance that faith brings, having our hearts sprinkled to cleanse us from a guilty conscience and having our bodies washed with pure water. Let us hold unswervingly to the hope we profess, for he who promised is faithful. And let us consider how we may spur one another on toward love and good deeds, not giving up meeting together, as some are in the habit of doing, but encouraging one another—and all the more as you see the Day approaching.

If we deliberately keep on sinning after we have received the knowledge of the truth, no sacrifice for sins is left, but only a fearful expectation of judgment and of raging fire that will consume the enemies of God.

"Anyone who rejected the law of Moses died without mercy on the testimony of two or three witnesses. How much more severely do you think someone deserves to be punished who has trampled the Son of God underfoot, who has treated as an unholy thing the blood of the covenant that sanctified them, and who has insulted the Spirit of grace? For we know him who said, "It is mine to avenge; I will repay," and again, "The Lord will judge his people."
It is a dreadful thing to fall into the hands of the living God.
Remember those earlier days after you had received the light, when you endured in a great conflict full of suffering. Sometimes you were publicly exposed to insult and persecution; at other times you stood side by side with those who were so treated. 34 You suffered along

with those in prison and joyfully accepted the confiscation of your property, because you knew that you yourselves had better and lasting possessions." Hebrews 10:19-34

MY NOTES

For this very reason, make every effort to add to your faith virtue; and to virtue, knowledge and to knowledge self-control and to self-control, perseverance and to perseverance, godliness and to godliness, brotherly kindness; and to brotherly kindness, love…..
2 Peter1:5-7 Berean Study Bible

Rest in the LORD and wait patiently for him: fret not thyself because of him who prospereth in his way, because of the man who bringeth wicked devices to pass. Psalm 37:7 (NKJ)

Persevere

Through Difficult Times
Through Trials
Through Losses

Lord, Help Me To Persevere!

MY NOTES

What is your plan? Set a goal.

You might be amazed by the immense array of accomplishments that await you once you establish clear goals and eliminate those pesky distractions that crowd your mind. I've often reflected on countless instances where I longed to embark on a particular task, only to be derailed by the relentless tide of daily life—because, in those moments, I either hadn't delineated my objectives, failed to clear out the noise around me, or simply lacked the willpower to push through. It's a truth universally acknowledged that when we meticulously devise our plans, we are poised to achieve far more. When we attune ourselves to the divine guidance that lays out our paths, our endeavors not only flourish but align beautifully with the purpose intended for us.

So, I ask you again:

WHAT IS YOUR PLAN?

WHAT ACTION STEPS WILL YOU TAKE TO MOVE
FORWARD?

And let's not overlook—WHAT IS HOLDING YOU BACK FROM TAKING THOSE STEPS
TODAY?

As we dig deeper, let's examine the myriad of obstacles that seem
to spring up and hinder our progress.

Living Intentional.

MY NOTES

11

DISTRACTIONS

Distractions arrive like unwelcome guests, purposefully designed to knock you off your carefully crafted balance and lead you down a path to failure. To illustrate my point, consider this: even the most experienced and steadfast Christians can find themselves at the mercy of these diversions, thrown off their spiritual equilibrium in moments of vulnerability.

The truth is, no one escapes this reality. Imagine a life where everything seems to be unfolding in perfect harmony, where the best-case scenario gleams brightly in your mind like a guiding star. And yet, just when you feel secure, the enemy—a cunning adversary— pulls back the bowstring, launching yet another dart aimed at your heart.

This seemingly innocuous attack can send the strongest among us spiraling, causing a sudden collapse that leads to doubt and despair. But remember, this moment of falling is not an invitation to remain on the ground. It is not an ending but merely a setback, a challenge to rise again. The call is to harness the strength within, to push through the fog of distractions with renewed determination, and to reclaim your footing on the path to victory.

After all, resilience is forged in the fire of adversity, and each distraction offers not just a test, but also the chance to grow stronger and more resolute.

The godly may trip seven times, but they will getup again. But one disaster is enough to overthrow the wicked. Proverbs 24:16

Many are the afflictions of the righteous, but the LORD delivers him from them all. Psalm 34:19

What are Distractions?

The instant God ignites a dream or a vision deep within your soul, it becomes vital to understand that this spark of divine inspiration will inevitably draw the attention of the enemy, Satan himself. He will unleash an arsenal of schemes and distractions, meticulously crafted to sidetrack you from the glorious path laid out for you. As you embark on this journey to fulfill your destiny, expect cunning plots and insidious whispers that seek to confuse your purpose and lead you astray, pulling you into a web of doubt and despair. Guard your heart and mind, for the fight to realize your God-given potential is not only a pursuit of joy but also a battle against the forces aimed at thwarting your every step.

What on this list of distractions trouble you?
Are any of these issues weighing heavily on your mind?

Comparisons
Brokenness
Pride
Disobedience
Pain
Lack of Focus
Double-Mindedness
Relationships
Family
An Offended Heart
People
Time
Lack of Direction
Fear

Faithful and trustworthy is He who is calling you [to Himself for your salvation], and He will do it [He will fulfill His call by making you holy, guarding you, watching over you, and protecting you as His own]. Amp. I Thessalonians 5:24

Lord, Teach Me To Know and Recognize my Distractions!

WHAT HAVE BEEN YOUR DISTRACTIONS? LIST THEM ON THIS PAGE.

If we are thrown into the blazing furnace, the God we serve can deliver us from it, and he will deliver us from Your Majesty's hand. Daniel 3:17

He has delivered us from such a deadly peril, and He will deliver us. In Him we have placed our hope that He will yet again deliver us. 2 Corinthians 1:10

The LORD is my light and my salvation--whom shall, I fear? The LORD is the stronghold of my life~whom shall I dread? Psalm 27:1,3

In this vast expanse of life, there exists truly nothing to fear—neither the haunting grip of sickness nor the unsettling specter of financial ruin, nor the dread of an empty pantry. NOT A SINGLE THING! This world may throw its challenges your way, testing the very fabric of your resolve, but when you are consciously living a life steeped in righteousness and integrity, you can boldly stand firm, assured of the countless promises that grace your path from a higher power. You will find that amidst the trials and tribulations, a profound peace envelops you, guiding your steps through the shadows of uncertainty with unwavering faith.

What, then, shall we say in response to these things? If God is for us, who can be against us? Romans 8:31 NIV

Israel, how happy you are! There is no one like you, a nation saved by the LORD. The LORD himself is your shield and your sword, to defend you and give you victory. Your enemies will come begging for mercy,
and you will trample them down. Deuteronomy 33:29

God stands unwavering at your side, a steadfast guardian against the chaos of life. He embodies the might of a shield, ever-present to deflect the arrows of doubt and fear. As a decisive sword, He cuts through the shadows with clarity, illuminating your path toward a brighter tomorrow. He is your ultimate salvation, waiting to embrace you in moments of despair, your enduring strength, lending you courage when you feel weak. In His embrace, you find a serene comforter, quieting the storms within your heart, and a profound peace that blankets your spirit like a gentle whisper.

Truly, He is your EVERYTHING. In the face of life's relentless distractions, know that God stands firmly, vigilant against every assault on your focus and resolve. As challenges mount and temptations arise to pull you away from your purpose, remember, He is your armor.

With His divine providence wrapping around you, you can FOCUS FORWARD! Let the noise of the world fade into silence, as you arm yourself with faith and determination, propelled by the unwavering presence of your Almighty ally.

Not that I have already obtained all this, or have already been made perfect, but I press on to take hold of which Christ Jesus took hold of me 13Brothers, I do not consider myself yet to have taken hold of it. But one thing I do: Forgetting what is behind and straining toward what is ahead, … Philippians 3:12-13

MY NOTES

12

GOAL SETTING

When I was just a little girl, the bright skies and the buzz of the airport fascinated me. I dreamed of becoming a flight attendant, a glamorous figure soaring through the clouds. My father would often take my sister and me to the bustling old Newark Airport in Newark, New Jersey where the scent of jet fuel mingled with excitement. We would sit for hours, eyes wide with wonder, captivated by the parade of passengers with their bags, emotions, and stories, boarding their flights. I reveled in watching the mighty aircraft land gracefully and then burst forth into the sky, with those elegant women in their crisp uniforms embodying grace and adventure.

As I reflect now, it strikes me as strange that no one ever really encouraged me to think beyond the confines of high school—no one ever suggested I should nurture ambitions of entrepreneurship or aspire to be a president of a company, let alone a flight attendant. Other than the books that my aunt provided from the library and the antique National Geographic magazines I read in my grandfather's attic did I envision my life as anything but a tapestry of dreams woven from my imagination. I drifted through the coming years, often guided by the whims of fate rather than my own aspirations. The trials I faced came at me like unexpected storms.

There were marriages—one joyful, others heart-wrenching—miscarriages that left me empty, a series of disappointments that nagged at my spirit. I navigated through the hectic worlds of school, ministry, and the exhausting demands of motherhood, while juggling various jobs, a slew of surgeries, and the incessant distractions life threw my way. Those diversions happened largely because I had no concrete plans; I lacked meaningful goals to anchor my ambitions. Instead of steering the course of my own destiny, I let life's circumstances decide my path. However, a profound awakening came when I embarked on a journey through the pages of the Bible, discovering the purpose imbued in my existence through its teachings. The joy I found was resplendent, particularly through the eyes of my children, the fulfillment of my ministry, and the woven narrative of life unfolding around me. Yet, without well-defined goals, I felt as if life merely happened to me, rolling along like an unexplored river, or so I believed.

I began my journey into seminary life in 1997, enveloped in the ancient languages of Hebrew and Greek as I pursued a master's degree in theology. I realize that God has quite the sense of humor because this was never part of my plan! Here I was, balancing the beautiful chaos of being a mother to three beautiful adopted children while serving as First Lady and an ordained pastor. It's almost laughable to think how unaware I was of the remarkable twists and turns that awaited me!

Fast forward to 2003, I found myself at a PCUSA conference in Oregon, engaging with an inspiring group of women. It was in that sacred space, amidst shared stories and spiritual exploration, that I heard the unmistakable voice of the Lord. He made it abundantly clear: despite my hesitation to pursue my dreams and the lack of goals I had laid out in my earlier years, I was undeniably living out a purpose that had been carefully crafted by His hand. I graduated from seminary the following year.
It wasn't until I turned sixty that my dream to become a flight attendant for a major airline finally soared to life. Though the journey had seemed prolonged, my aspirations were gradually realized in the most unexpected of ways. I had transformed into a SKYANGEL! The coveted position I once only dared to envision was now a tangible reality. What I had dismissed as mere distractions in the tapestry of my life turned out to be divine interventions, leading me down a path of preparation and growth.

God yearns for you to dream boldly, to cultivate an ambition that mirrors the vastness of your potential. He has brought forth my own desires, knowing well the intricate tapestry of my life story. Picture the tallest skyscraper imaginable, with God perched atop, surveying the entirety of your journey from beginning to end.
Amid the inevitable heartbreak, challenges, and setbacks, He possesses the wisdom to guide you toward fulfillment. This book stands as a testament to that divine fulfillment. Time and again, when I sought His guidance, He brought me toward my airline aspirations. In His infinite wisdom, He orchestrated the perfect timing to fulfill that career dream in my life. That longing crystallized into reality because of His leading hand and perfect timing.

I will stand at my watch and station myself on the ramparts.I will look to see what he will say to me, and what answer I am to give to this complaint. The Lord's Answer Then the Lord replied: "Write down the revelation and make it plain on tablets so that a herald may run with it. For the revelation awaits an appointed time. It speaks of the end and will not

prove false. Though it lingers, wait for it. It will certainly come and will not delay.
Habakkuk 2:1-3 (NIV)

It is your destiny—a profound revelation that reverberates through your very soul. God urges you to take up the pen and etch your thoughts, your dreams into the fabric of existence. Share it widely; let your voice be a beacon for others navigating their own paths. Engrave your vision upon the stubborn stone of time. For my own destiny, it was written deep within my heart and spirit, whispering its truths to me in quiet moments. Had I committed it to paper more earnestly, had I nurtured it by sharing it with the world, perhaps it would have flourished sooner, untouched by the corrosive influences of time, discouragement, or the skepticism of others, all of which can shroud the light of your dreams in shadow. So I ask you now, in the quiet of your mind, what is your vision? What are the goals that ignite your spirit? What dreams do you hold close, waiting for the moment they can be unleashed upon the world? Reflect deeply upon these questions, for they are the keys to unlock the doors of your potential.

Do You Set Ambitious Goals?

Establishing clear objectives is essential for successfully achieving them.

I press on toward the goal to win the prize for which God has called me heavenward in Christ Jesus. Philippians 3:15

Whatsoever things are lovely...think on these things. Philippians 4:8

GOALS

Number and list your goals from the previous page in order of importance. Which of the goals are you going to do today?

CREATE A LIST AND AFFIRM HOW YOU'RE GOING TO TACKLE EACH ITEM. BE PRAGMATIC.

WHICH OF YOUR ASPIRATIONS WILL YOU PURSUE THIS WEEK?

CREATE A LIST AND AFFIRM HOW YOU'RE GOING TO TACKLE EACH ITEM. BE PRAGMATIC.

WHICH OF YOUR ASPIRATIONS WILL YOU FOCUS ON THIS MONTH?

CREATE A LIST AND AFFIRM HOW YOU'RE GOING TO TACKLE EACH ITEM. BE PRAGMATIC.

WHAT GOALS DO YOU ENVISION ACCOMPLISHING THIS YEAR?

TAKE A MOMENT TO WRITE THEM DOWN AND STRATEGIZE HOW YOU WILL BRING THEM TO LIFE.

BE PRAGMATIC. STAY GROUNDED IN REALITY.

WHAT AMBITIONS WILL YOU STRIVE TO ACHIEVE IN THE COMING FIVE YEARS?
JOT THEM DOWN AND DEVISE A PLAN OF HOW YOU INTEND TO REALIZE THEM.

Be pragmatic. Stay grounded in your aspirations.

PRAY

STAND STRONG

13

KEEPING YOUR FOCUS FORWARD

Not that I have already obtained this or am already perfect, but I press on to make it my own, because Jesus Christ has made me his own. Philippians 3:12 ESV

Reflect on that time when you felt the divine presence most vividly in your life.

What changed during that period?

Consider your interactions in public, your achievements in your profession, and the quiet moments in your private life.

Write those down and PRAY

DECLARE AND DECREE

I can do ALL things through Christ who strengthens me!

FOCUS

It is the only way to keep your goals clearer than your mistakes!

PRAY

Lord,
Be My Focus!

14

AM I DISCIPLINED?

Now that we have a clear understanding of our focus and have articulated what we truly desire, it becomes paramount to prioritize not only our motivation but also our discipline as we move forward on this journey.

Discipline is an extraordinary tool; it far surpasses the fleeting nature of mere motivation. While motivation often requires an external nudge, an encouraging word, or an inspiring quote to invigorate action,
discipline operates on an entirely diverse realm.

Discipline embodies a deep-seated commitment within myself—an unwavering promise that I don't rely on any external force to spur me into action. It's an intrinsic quality that defines my ethos, seamlessly woven into the very fabric of my being. It's akin to the daily ritual of rising from bed, brushing my teeth, and dressing for the day ahead—simple actions that are now instinctual and automatic.

Many of us embark on the path of habit formation with fervor, only to cast aside our efforts when immediate results remain elusive. There's a timeless truth hidden in the adage that it takes thirty days to establish a new habit; it's not merely a catchy phrase, but a reminder that patience is a crucial companion
on the road to reinvention.

Habits demand time and consistent effort to transform into intrinsic facets of our identity. Just as the ancient saying goes, "Rome wasn't built in a day," the cultivation of any new skill, mindset, or habit is a process that unfolds gradually, brick by brick.

Consider the day when you first learned the importance of brushing your teeth twice a day. Initially, it may have felt like an obtrusive chore, something that required conscious thought and effort. Over time, however, you began to grasp the significance of dental hygiene and its crucial role in maintaining a healthy mouth.

The routine became second nature, deeply embedded in your daily rituals. Now, the act of brushing your teeth has become a seamless part of your life, a habitual action performed without thought or hesitation. It's a testament to the power of discipline, illustrating how over time, what was once an effort transforms into an instinctive, essential part of your daily routine.

DISCIPLINES

Disciplines are a practice which helps to train your behavior.

Disciplines help to
define goals,
commit,
avoid temptation,
take care of themselves,
develop habits,
set boundaries,
revel in routine,
and help keep your focus.
I must be intentional about my practices.

DECLARE and DECREE

I am disciplined by the Word of God.

MY NOTES

DISCIPLINE

I remember the day I finally caved and paused my rigorous physical training, a dedication that had spanned six solid months. The fruits of my labor were apparent; muscles were sculpting beautifully, and I could feel the vitality coursing through me. I was gaining strength, my body shedding layers of fat, revealing the leaner, healthier me beneath. It was a euphoric experience until, unexpectedly, illness struck. I developed a nasty case of bronchitis that confined me to my bed for three long, monotonous days. Each passing hour felt like an eternity, and the gym—the place where I felt empowered and alive—became a distant memory.

My discipline wavered as I debated the value of returning to my routine versus allowing myself the grace of recovery. Weeks trickled by, days blended together, and I found myself in an uncomfortable limbo, yearning for the sense of accomplishment that came with every rep and every drop of sweat. At last, gathering my willpower, I steeled myself to start anew. However, I discovered that muscles, resilient as ever, harbor a kind of memory. The instant I stepped back into my workout regimen, it was as if they were just waiting for me to return. Each lift felt familiar, and I effortlessly resumed my previous momentum, the echo of my former strength gently beckoning me back. With renewed energy and determination, I embraced the grind once more, and all was well.

Good disciplines are contagious.

Ways To Keep my Disciplines Consistent
Join a Bible believing, Word teaching church
Believe God for what you are doing.

Train with other goal setters.

Socialize with others who are already
accomplishing what you are
attempting to do.

Practice Daily.

Don't stop.

(It takes a lifetime to build disciplines, if you stop, they stop!)

Lord, teach me how to be disciplined

MY NOTES

MY NOTES

MY NOTES

BE
BRAVE

Be Courageous

Creative

Dream

Explore

Inspire

Be Limitless

Unstoppable

Have Strength

Find Your Purpose

Be Intentional

MY PRAYER

15

LORD, TEACH ME TO HAVE NO FEAR

Lord,
I am afraid.
Teach me to have NO FEAR!
Don't be afraid, for I am with you.
Don't be discouraged, for I am God.
I will strengthen you and help you.
I will hold you up with my victorious right hand.
Isaiah 41:10

DECLARE and DECREE
I will have no fear!

When you pass through the waters, I will be with you; and when you pass through the rivers, they will not sweep over you. When you walk through the fire, you will not be burned; the flames will not set you ablaze. For I am the Lord your God ... Isaiah 43:2-3 NIV

STAY FEARLESS

What fears linger in your heart that you believe God has not already vanquished from your
life?

When you earnestly call out to Him, He answers with a powerful arsenal of support,
equipping you to confront and halt the enemy in his tracks. Just as David stood against
Goliath armed with faith and a slingshot, you too can draw upon divine strength to crush all
doubts and struggles that loom ahead.

Recall the resolve of Daniel, who faced hungry lions with unwavering courage, and the trio
of Shadrach, Meshach, and Abednego, who boldly entered the blazing furnace, trusting
their God to deliver them. Their stories serve not merely as tales from ancient times, but as
living testaments to the unshakeable might of faith in the face of formidable challenges.

Transform your fears into a catalyst for courage, embracing the immense power of God that
flows through you to protect and guide you, liberating you from the snares of the adversary.
Never underestimate the sheer force of prayer; it remains the most formidable weapon in
your arsenal.

Each time the enemy encroaches upon your peace, seeking to undermine your purpose or
identity, remind him with conviction that he is already humbled and defeated. In the name
of Jesus, there is no power he possesses
that can inflict harm upon you.

As you begin to call upon His holy name, behold as the very atmosphere around you
transforms, a palpable shift igniting the power of change. So step forward with audacity,
and accept the challenge to be BOLD in Jesus' name, for with Him, victory is not just
possible—it is assured.

You say you have faith, for you believe that there is one God. Good for you! Even the demons believe this, and they tremble in terror. James 2:19

Demons quake in fear at the mere whisper of His name, especially as we begin to ignite the vibrant flame of our faith in our Lord. When we fervently call upon the wondrous and awe-inspiring name of Jesus—oh, how it reverberates through the heavens—we unleash the boundless power of God across the earth, tearing down strongholds and thwarting every wicked scheme the enemy has intricately woven into our lives. These demons may find themselves entrapped by the deceitful whispers of Satan, but deep down, they tremble in recognition of the undeniable superiority of God's omnipotent might. In our steadfast faith and resolute belief, we become beacons of light, casting shadows that dissolve the dark treachery of despair. Through our unwavering trust in His name, we forge a path of victory, rendering the plans of the adversary futile while elevating the glory of His kingdom here on earth.

Why should you fear the enemy when he has absolutely NO power over you?

Whereas demons believe in God and know Him, many humans on the other hand still struggle to believe in His existence, let alone acknowledge His omniscient power. "He (Jesus) was amazed at their lack of faith."
Mark 6:6

As you yield your emotions, thoughts, and actions to God's will, your offering will ignite your FAITH; in turn, your belief will fuel you with encouragement and resilience.

As for God, his way is perfect:

The Lord's word is flawless.
he shields all who take refuge in him.

For who is God besides the Lord?

And who is the Rock except our God?

It is God who arms me with strength
and keeps my way secure.

He makes my feet like the feet of a deer;
he causes me to stand on the heights.

Psalm 18:30-33

Truly my soul finds rest in God;
my salvation comes from him.

Truly he is my rock and my salvation;
he is my fortress, I will never be shaken.

How long will you assault me?

Would all of you throw me down —
this leaning wall, this tottering fence?

Surely they intend to topple me
from my lofty place;
they take delight in lies.

With their mouths they bless,
but in their hearts they curse.

Yes, my soul, find rest in God;
my hope comes from him.

Truly he is my rock and my salvation;
he is my fortress, I will not be shaken.

My salvation and my honor depend on God;
he is my mighty rock, my refuge.

Trust in him at all times, you people;
pour out your hearts to him,
for God is our refuge.

Psalm 62:1-8

ABOUT THE AUTHOR

Pastor Valari Knight Boston stands as a beacon of hope and inspiration, an ordained minister whose heart beats for the gospel. A seasoned certified executive and grief coach, she breathes life into every conference she speaks at, sharing profound personal testimonies that illuminate the boundless love of Christ to every soul she encounters. With a profound command of the fivefold gifts, she masterfully weaves Scriptural truths into her teachings, diligently working to uplift the congregation and draw souls closer to the kingdom.

Endowed with the spirit of intercession, Pastor Val, as she is affectionately known, has founded numerous women's bible studies, empowering women for over three decades through her dedicated ministries. Her powerful sermons have echoed in various conferences across the globe, from the vibrant streets of Lagos, Nigeria, Kinshasa in the Democratic Republic of Congo to the cultural heart of Paris, France, spanning Brussels, Belgium, Quebec, Canada, and various venues throughout the United States.

An esteemed graduate of Gordon Conwell Theological Seminary in Charlotte, Pastor Valari carries her academic achievements gracefully. In her personal life, she is a former flight attendant whose heart has landed in the embrace of her husband, Val Boston III. Together, they celebrate the journey of parenthood with five adult children and take joy in their roles as grandparents to nine cherished grandchildren.

To learn more about Valari Knight Boston
we invite you to log onto her website:

www.VKBMinistries.com

or write her at

ResilientCoachV@gmail.com